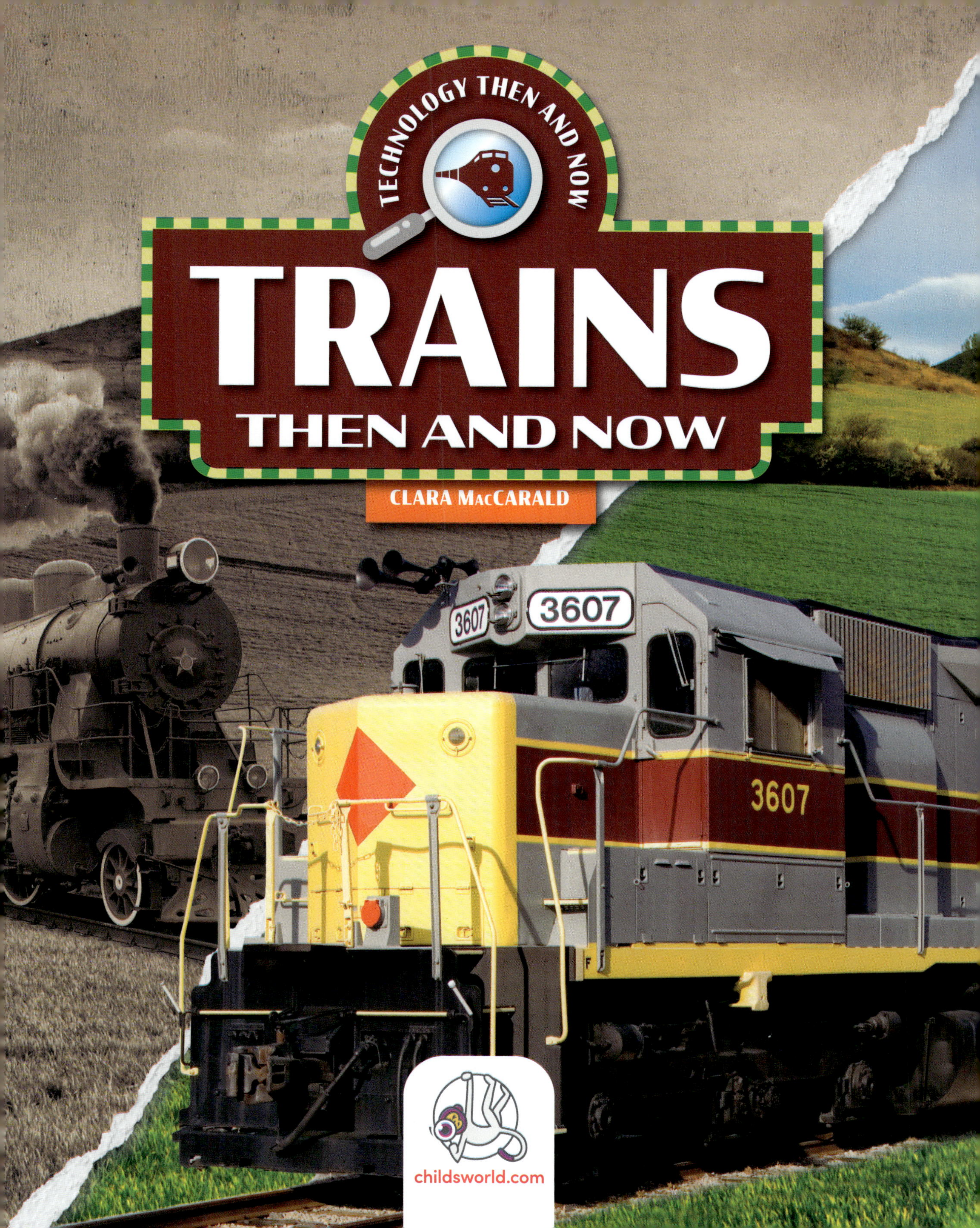
TECHNOLOGY THEN AND NOW
TRAINS
THEN AND NOW
CLARA MacCARALD
3607
3607
3607
childsworld.com

Published by The Child's World®
800-599-READ • www.childsworld.com

Photography Credits
Photographs ©: Dmitry Eliuseev/Shutterstock Images, cover (old train), 1 (old train); Jiri Ambroz/Shutterstock Images, cover (background), 1 (background), 3 (background); Shutterstock Images, cover (modern train), cover (smoke), cover (icon), 1 (modern train), 1 (smoke), 1 (icon), 3 (icon), 4, 7, 17, 18, 22; Natalya Temnaya/Shutterstock Images, 5; Kev Gregory/Shutterstock Images, 8; Zack Frank/Shutterstock Images, 10–11; Grand Warszawski/Shutterstock Images, 12–13; Ian Dewar Photography/Shutterstock Images, 14; Cyo Bo/Shutterstock Images, 20

ISBN Information
9781503889545 (Reinforced Library Binding)
9781503891166 (Portable Document Format)
9781503892408 (Online Multi-user eBook)
9781503893641 (Electronic Publication)

LCCN 2023950463

Printed in the United States of America

Clara MacCarald is a freelance writer with a master's degree in ecology and natural resources. She lives with her family in an off-grid house nestled in the forests of central New York. When not parenting her daughter, she spends her time writing nonfiction books for kids.

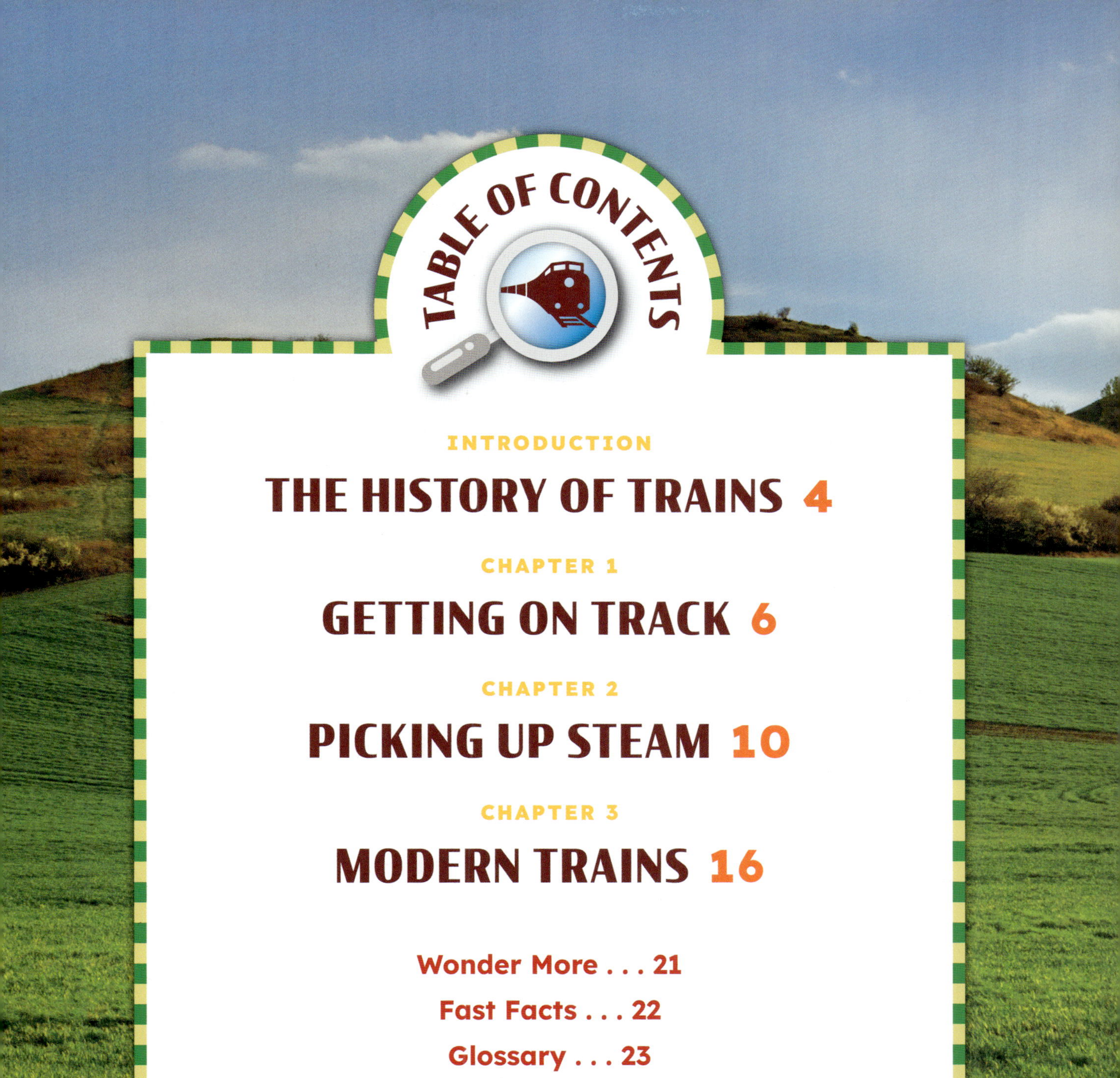
TABLE OF CONTENTS

TRAINS

Trains are lines of railroad cars connected together. Trains are often pulled on a railway track by a **locomotive**. People built the first railways around 600 BC. Inventing locomotives took much longer. The first locomotive ran on a railway in 1803.

Today, there are trains all around the world. Trains can haul goods. The average **freight** train in the United States is more than 1 mile (1.6 km) long. Trains can move almost any kind of product. They can haul grain, oil, and even airplane parts. Some train cars act like refrigerators. They can keep food cool or frozen.

Most passenger trains have windows to let passengers look outside.

Trains can also carry **passengers**. Amtrak is a US railroad company. Amtrak reported that almost 23 million passengers rode their trains in 2022. Trains are an important part of the modern world.

GETTING ON TRACK

Before there could be trains, people needed tracks. Ancient Greeks made a type of railway around 600 BC. They cut tracks into a road. Wheeled carts rolled along the tracks. The carts carried boats across a narrow strip of land. This railway was used for hundreds of years before it no longer worked.

It took a long time before people made the next railways. In the 1550s, Germans created wagonways. Two wooden rails were set side by side in the road. Horses could pull wagon wheels more easily over the rails than over dirt.

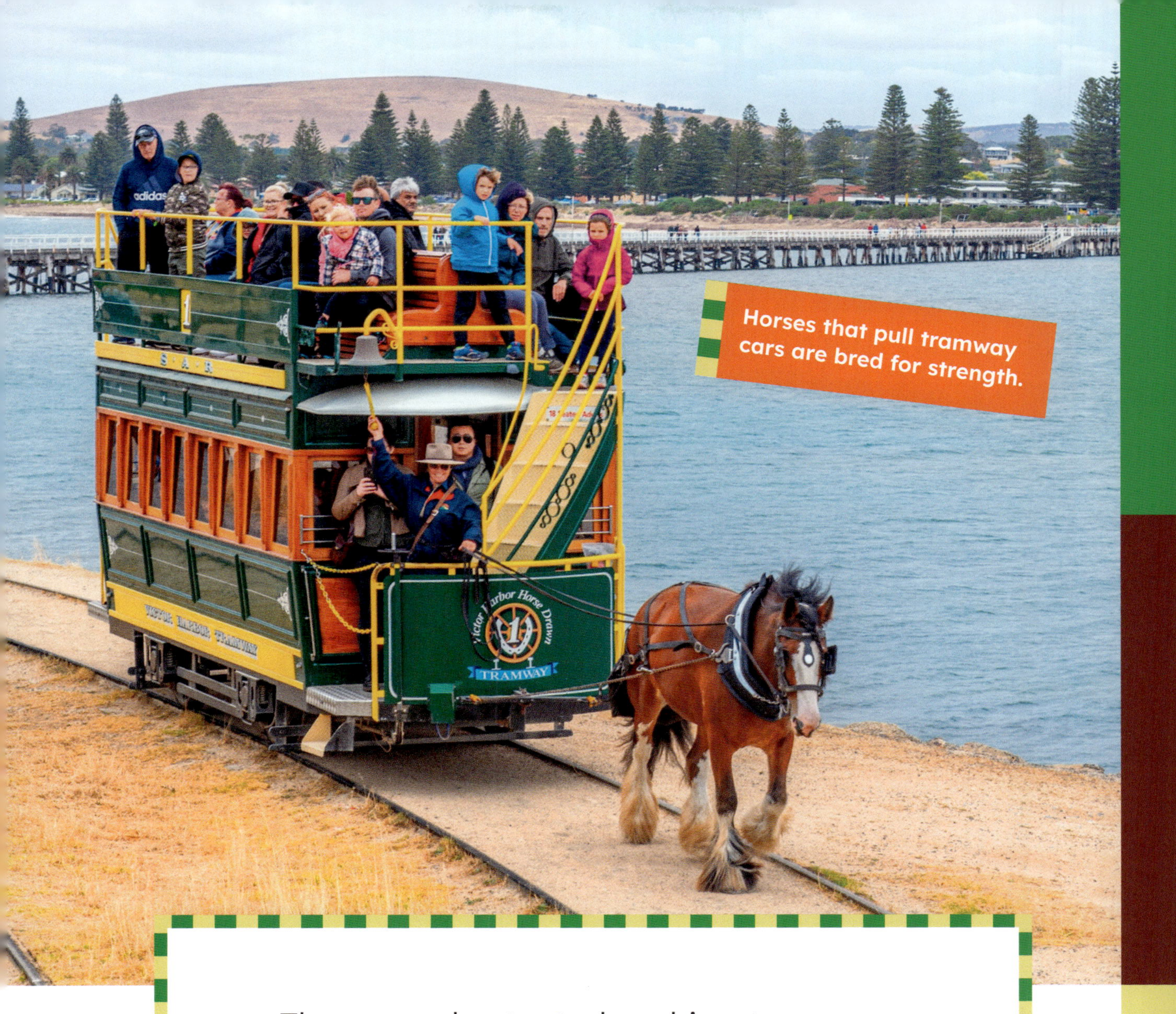

Horses that pull tramway cars are bred for strength.

Then people started making tramways. These were like wagonways but with iron rails. Tramway routes spread across Europe in the late 1700s. Horses still pulled the wagons.

A copy of the *Rocket* locomotive operates in England.

In 1803, British inventor Richard Trevithick built a locomotive. It had a steam engine. The steam engine burned coal to boil water. The swelling steam from the water powered the engine. Trevithick's locomotive was the first steam locomotive that could run on a railway. Unfortunately, it was too heavy. The rails were not strong enough to support the locomotive.

Businesses wanted better ways to move products and people quickly. Other inventors worked on new locomotives. Their inventions were all different. In 1829, officials at an English railway company decided to hold a contest. They wanted to find the best locomotive. Each locomotive that entered the contest ran ten times around a 1.5-mile (2.4-km) track. A locomotive named *Rocket* won. It was built by George and Robert Stephenson. *Rocket* became a model for other locomotives.

PICKING UP STEAM

Railroads and trains spread around the world. At first, locomotives traveled at speeds of around 30 miles per hour (48 kmh). They were about as fast as an average horse. Trains and tracks got better over time, so trains could move faster. By 1850, British trains reached speeds of 78 miles per hour (126 kmh).

On May 10, 1869, the east and west coasts of the United States were connected by railroad at this location in the state of Utah.

Some subway systems are built hundreds of feet underground.

Before trains, people moved large loads by water. People built **canals** where there was not a river or lake. But trains could carry more goods and move faster than canal boats. People began to build new railroads instead of new canals. In the 1860s, low-cost steel made railroads even cheaper to build.

Trains became more comfortable for passengers. People created new kinds of cars for sleeping and dining. New closed walkways let passengers walk safely between cars.

Steam power produced very dirty smoke. To control the smoke, people began building underground tunnels for trains in cities. These were the first **subways**.

THE PULLMAN SLEEPING CAR

George Pullman didn't invent the sleeping car. But he did make it fancier. In 1865, the Pullman sleeping car rode on train tracks for the first time. The walls and furniture inside it were beautiful. Seats could be used as comfortable beds. People loved to ride in his cars.

People also started using electric trains. The train track itself provided electricity to the train. The first train powered by an electric track ran in Berlin, Germany, in 1879. Electric tracks spread in the United States and Europe in the late 1800s and early 1900s.

In 1918, a car powered by **diesel** fuel ran on a railway for the first time. Diesel-electric locomotives followed. Their engines used diesel fuel to create electricity, which turned the wheels. Diesel-electric locomotives used less fuel than steam-powered trains. Railroads began changing to diesel-electric. Few steam locomotives remained by the late 1960s.

MODERN TRAINS

Trains and tracks continue to improve. In general, trains run much faster today than they did 100 years ago. Many countries have built high-speed rail lines. Trains on these rails carry passengers at speeds of 124 miles per hour (200 kmh) or more. Most high-speed trains are electric.

One of the world's fastest trains reaches speeds of 286 miles per hour (460 kmh) or more. It is called a Maglev train.

MAGNETIC FORCES

Opposite sides of magnets pull toward each other. Same sides push away. Maglev trains use these forces to lift the train and push it forward.

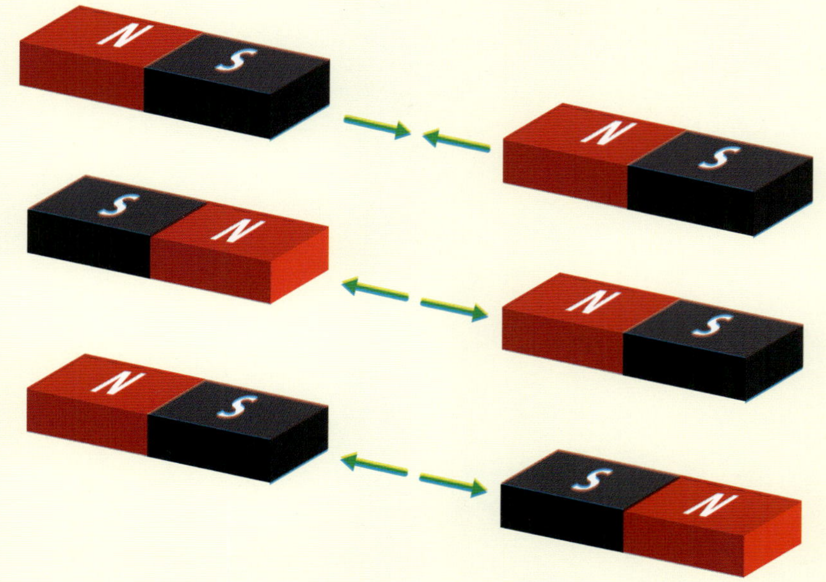

Maglev trains use the force of magnets to move the train along the track. The train does not touch the track. Instead, very strong magnets push the train about 5 inches (12.7 cm) above the track. Then other magnets make the train go forward.

SOLAR TRAINS

In 2017, a train in Australia called the Byron **Solar** Train started running. It carries solar panels on its roof. Solar panels are flat boards that capture energy from the sun to make electricity. The Byron Solar Train uses only solar power. In the future, other trains may use solar power, too.

This train has computers that help save fuel.

Computers have helped make modern trains safer. Computer systems can tell people when two trains are heading toward each other. A train's computer can hit the brake before the train runs into something. Computers can also keep trains from driving over speed limits.

Today, trains are also getting longer. Some freight trains stretch for 3 miles (4.8 km). But train crews are getting smaller. Some trains have no driver at all. These are called **automatic** trains. Computers drive the train. Sometimes there is one person on the train who can take over if the computer has a problem.

In 2023, the fastest train in the world was the Shanghai Maglev. Trains in the future could be even faster.

People are working to make automatic trains that run outside of cities. People also hope to build more high-speed rails. One day a train may travel between the east and west coasts of the United States in under 7 hours. Trains have changed a lot since the first locomotive. It is fun to think about how trains will change in the future.

WONDER MORE

Wondering about New Information

How much did you know about trains before reading this book? What new information did you learn? Write down three new facts that this book taught you. Was the new information surprising? Why or why not?

Wondering How It Matters

What is one way trains relate to your life? If you cannot think of a personal connection, imagine a way trains might affect other kids. What impact might trains have on their lives?

Wondering Why

Trains in cities are often underground. Why do you think people built them that way? Do you think there should be more trains running underground outside of cities? Why or why not?

Ways to Keep Wondering

The history of trains is a complex topic. After reading this book, what questions do you have about it? What can you do to learn more about trains?

FAST FACTS

- In the 1550s, people in Germany started making wagonways with two wooden rails side by side. Tramways, which had iron rails, spread across Europe in the 1700s.
- In 1803, Richard Trevithick made the first steam locomotive that could run on a railway.
- The first trains were about as fast as the average horse. Trains became faster as locomotives and tracks got stronger.
- In 1879, the first electric train ran in Germany.
- People invented diesel-electric locomotives in the early 1900s. Most railroads stopped using steam locomotives by the late 1960s.
- Today, high-speed rail lines have trains that travel more than 124 miles per hour (200 kmh).
- The fastest train in the world is a Maglev train. Magnets power Maglev trains.
- Computers make modern trains safer. They can stop a train or slow it down.
- Modern trains can be more than 3 miles (4.8 km) long.
- Some modern trains are automatic.

GLOSSARY

automatic (aw-tuh-MAT-ik) Something automatic can run without a person controlling it. Computers run automatic trains.

canals (kuh-NALZ) Canals are channels of water built through land to connect two bodies of water. People build canals to transport goods by boat.

diesel (DEE-zuhl) Diesel is a type of fuel similar to gasoline. Many trains run on diesel.

freight (FRAYT) Freight is goods that are transported. Some freight trains move food in cold cars.

locomotive (loh-kuh-MOH-tiv) A locomotive is an engine that pulls a train. The first locomotive was too heavy for the tracks of its day.

passengers (PASS-uhn-jurs) Passengers are people traveling in a vehicle who are not driving or working on it. Over time, trains became more comfortable for passengers.

solar (SOH-lur) Solar means having to do with the sun. Someday there may be more trains powered by solar energy.

subways (SUB-wayz) Subways are systems of trains running underground in a city. Many people take subways to work.

FIND OUT MORE

In the Library

Coiley, John. *Train.* New York, NY: DK, 2022.

Prénat, Sophie. *Trains.* San Francisco, CA: Chronicle Books, 2020.

Washburne, Sophie. *Great Train Designs.* New York, NY: Cavendish Square, 2023.

On the Web

Visit our website for links about trains:
childsworld.com/links

Note to Parents, Caregivers, Teachers, and Librarians: We routinely verify our web links to make sure they are safe and active sites. So encourage your readers to check them out!

INDEX